Staying Healthy:

Personal Safety

Alice B. McGinty

FRANKLIN WATTS
A DIVISION OF GROLIER PUBLISHING
NEW YORK / LONDON / HONG KONG / SYDNEY
DANBURY, CONNECTICUT

Book Design: Kim Sonsky

Photo Illustrations: Cover by Seth Dinnerman; pp. 20, 21 by Kelly Hahn; all photo illustrations by Seth Dinnerman.

Library of Congress Cataloging-in-Publication Data

McGinty, Alice B.
        Staying healthy. Personal safety / Alice B. McGinty.
            p.   cm. (The library of healthy living)
        Includes index.
        Summary: Gives children pointers on how to stay safe by thinking safe, including chapters on safety with strangers, friends, while playing, at home, and in the neighborhood.
        ISBN 0-531-11662-X
        1. Accidents—Prevention—Juvenile literature. 2. Safety education—Juvenile literature. 3. Drug abuse—Juvenile literature. 4. Children and strangers—Juvenile literature. [1. Safety.] I. Title. II. Series.
        HV675.5.M38 1997
        613.6—dc21   96-39985
                                                                                      CIP
                                                                                      AC

Contents

1   Learning About Safety   4

2   Think Safe, Act Safe   6

3   Staying Safe in Your Neighborhood   8

4   Thinking Safe at Home   10

5   Safety with Strangers   12

6   Keeping Your Body Safe   14

7   Staying Safe with Friends   16

8   Staying Safe While You Play   18

9   People Who Can Help You Stay Safe   20

10   Choose to Be Safe   22

   Glossary   23

   Index   24

Learning About Safety

You are growing up. You do many exciting things on your own. Maybe you ride a bike, go places with friends, or play without your mom or dad. These things are exciting, but they can also be **dangerous** (DAYN-jer-us).

Your parents work to keep you safe. They don't want you to get hurt or lost or to be scared.

Now that you are bigger, it is your job to learn about safety. It is an important part of taking care of yourself.

Wearing a helmet when you ride your bike is a good way to show your parents that you know how important safety is. ▶

Think Safe, Act Safe

To be safe, you need to think safe. Thinking safe means being **aware** (uh-WAYR) of things that can hurt you.

Let's say you see a drawer open. Think safe first. Ask yourself, "What could happen?" The answer is that you or someone else could bump into the drawer and get hurt.

Then, be safe. Close the drawer. This will **prevent** (pre-VENT), or stop, **accidents** (AK-sih-dents) from happening.

When you think safe, you help to keep yourself safe from harm.

By thinking and acting safely, you can keep accidents from happening. ▶

Staying Safe in Your Neighborhood

Sometimes people make safety rules to help you think safe. Your parents may have several rules for when you play in your **neighborhood** (NAY-ber-hood). These may include rules such as don't play outside after dark, don't talk to people you don't know, and make sure a parent knows where you are at all times.

Do you ride a bike in your neighborhood? Follow traffic and other bike safety rules. For example: Wear a helmet, watch for holes

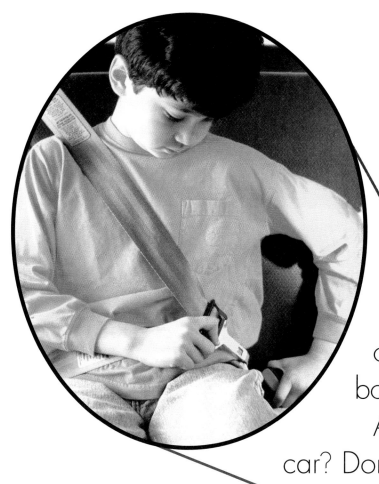

in the street, and never carry anyone on your bike.

Are you going to walk somewhere? Remember to cross streets at corners or at crosswalks and to look both ways for cars and bikes. Are you going to ride in a car? Don't forget to fasten your seat belt!

Following safety rules will help you stay safe in your neighborhood.

Thinking Safe at Home

Many things at home are **poisonous** (POY-zun-us), such as cleaners, weed killers, and plant foods and plants.

Poisons can make you sick if you eat or drink them. Think safe. Ask yourself, "Is this food?" If it isn't, don't put it in your mouth.

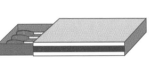

Stoves, ovens, and matches can cause burns and start fires. Outlets and

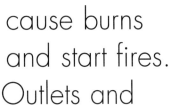

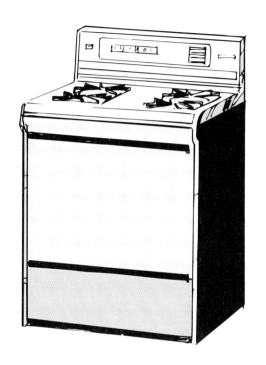

electrical appliances (ee-LEK-trih-kul uh-PLY-en-sez) can shock you and start fires. Think safe. Ask your parents to teach you about fire and electrical safety rules.

Knives and sharp tools are dangerous. Think safe. Stay away from things that can hurt you.

Safety with Strangers

A **stranger** (STRAYN-jer) is someone you don't know. Many strangers are nice. But some strangers only pretend to be nice. They may try to hurt you. How can you stay safe around strangers?

☺ If you're home alone, keep the doors locked. If a stranger comes to your house, do not answer the door.

☺ If a stranger calls on the phone, do not tell him or her if you are home alone. You can say, "My mom can't come to the phone right now." Then tell an adult that a stranger called.

☺ If a stranger offers you a ride or a present, run away.

☺ Never go anywhere with a stranger! He or she may hurt you.

You can't tell which strangers are mean and which are nice by the way they look or act.

13

Keeping Your Body Safe

Your body belongs to you. What should you do if someone tries to hurt you or touches you in a way that makes you feel bad or scared? Protect yourself. Yell "No!" and run away, even if that person is someone you know.

Nobody should hurt you or touch you in ways that you do not like, no matter who they are. If this happens to you, tell your parents or another adult you can trust right away.

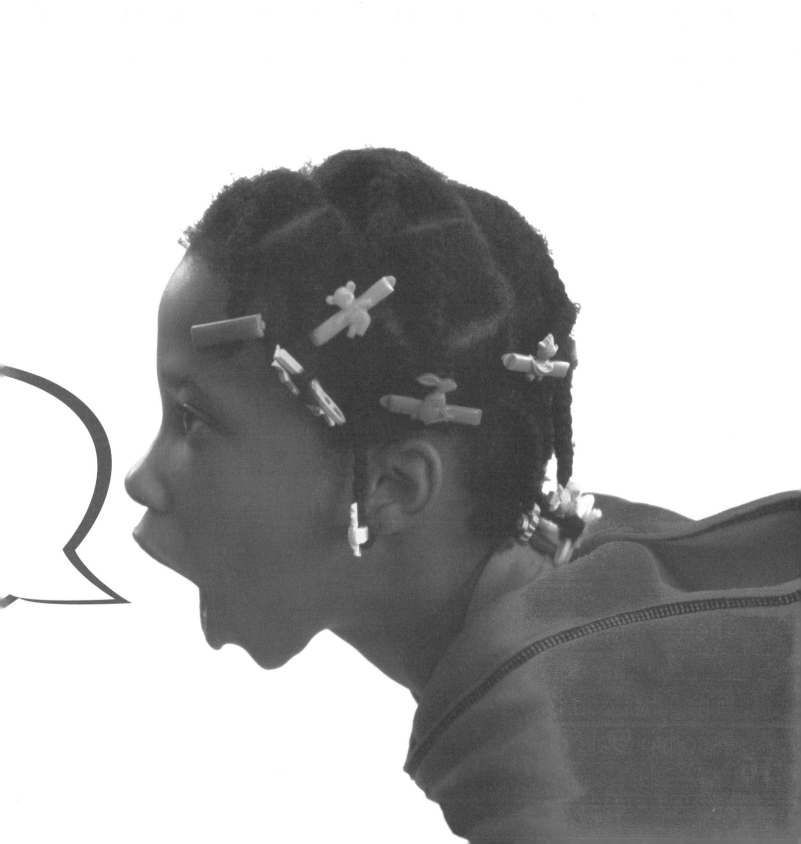

Staying Safe with Friends

Friends do many fun things together. But some of those things may be dangerous. A friend may say something like, "Try this trick on your bike," or "Let's explore these woods."

Think safe. Ask yourself these questions: "Is this dangerous?" "Could I get lost?" "Could I hurt myself or someone else?" If the answer to any of these questions is yes, don't do it. It is not safe.

A friend may offer you **drugs** (DRUGZ), **alcohol** (AL-kuh-hawl), **cigarettes** (SIG-uh-rets), or someone else's **medicine** (MED-ih-sin). He may tell you that these things will make you feel good. But they won't. These things hurt your body.

You choose what *you* do. Be safe. Say "no" to things that can hurt you or make you feel uncomfortable or scared.

Staying Safe While You Play

Many fun things have rules to help you play safely.

Do you like to swim? Learn the water safety rules. Make sure there is always a **lifeguard** (LYF-gard) or an adult with you. Also, it is important to wear sunscreen to prevent sunburn.

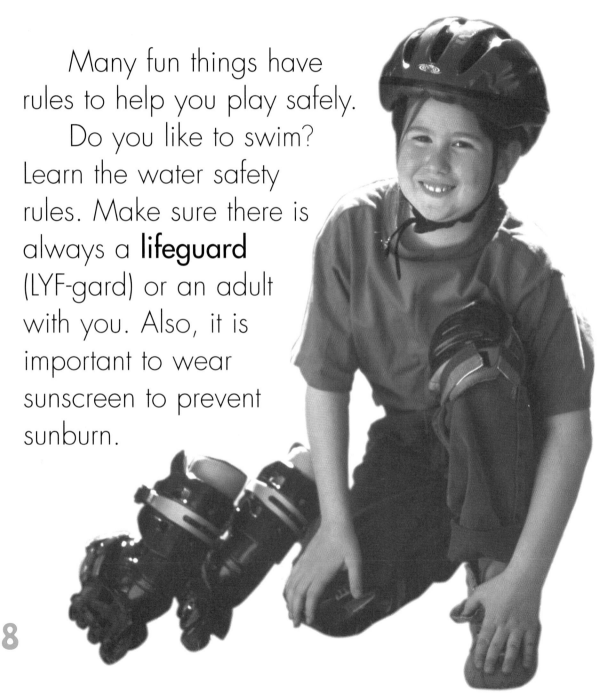

When you play on your own or with friends, make sure that you wear the right safety **gear** (GEER). If you go in-line skating, wear a helmet, wrist guards, and knee pads. If you ride your bike, wear a helmet.

If you play sports, such as baseball, soccer, or football, your coach will teach you the safety rules. He or she will also make sure you wear the right safety gear for that sport. If you play baseball, wear a helmet when it's your turn at bat. If you play soccer, wear shin guards. If you play football, wear shoulder pads and knee pads.

It's important to follow the safety rules even when your coach is not there. Stay **alert** (uh-LERT) while you play to prevent accidents.

People Who Can Help You Stay Safe

Even when you try to be safe, accidents sometimes happen anyway. What should you do if you or someone else gets hurt or needs help? Stay calm and think. Then go for help. There are people who can help you. You can ask your parents, the police, store clerks, crossing guards, and firefighters for

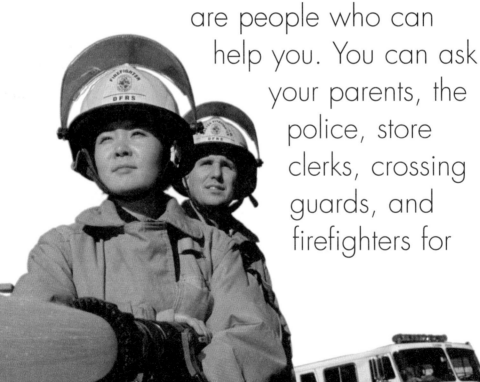

help. Neighbors can help too if your parents are not there.

Keep **emergency** (ee-MER-jen-see) phone numbers by the phone so you can get help fast.

21

Choose to Be Safe

You can choose to be safe in many ways. Stay away from dangerous places, especially at night or if you are alone. Whenever you leave your house, remember to tell someone where you are going. Whatever you may do, think safe. Learn the safety rules and follow them. Be aware of dangerous things and things that might cause accidents. Ask yourself "think safe" questions before you try something new.

Take care of yourself!

Glossary

accident (AK-sih-dent) Something harmful or unlucky that happens all of a sudden.

alcohol (AL-kuh-hawl) Something in beer, wine, and liquor that changes the way you think, feel, and act.

alert (uh-LERT) Aware.

aware (uh-WAYR) Knowing what is going on around you.

cigarette (SIG-uh-ret) Dried tobacco that is rolled in paper and smoked.

dangerous (DAYN-jer-us) Causing harm.

drug (DRUG) Something that changes the way you feel, think, and act.

electrical appliances (ee-LEK-trih-kul uh-PLY-en-sez) Machines that are run by electricity.

emergency (ee-MER-jen-see) A sudden need for quick action.

gear (GEER) What you wear to stay safe while playing sports.

lifeguard (LYF-gard) A person whose job is to keep people safe in the water.

medicine (MED-ih-sin) Drug that can help a person get well if he is sick.

neighborhood (NAY-ber-hood) The area in which you live.

poisonous (POY-zun-us) When something has poison in it and that can harm you.

prevent (pre-VENT) To stop.

stranger (STRAYN-jer) A person you don't know.

Index

A
accidents, 6, 19, 20
    preventing, 6, 19
alcohol, 16
alert, being, 19
aware, being, 6

B
bike, riding a, 4, 8, 9,
    16, 19
body, your, 14, 16

C
cigarettes, 16

D
danger, 4, 11, 16, 22
drugs, 16

E
electrical appliances,
    10–11
emergency phone
    numbers, 21

F
fires, 10, 11
friends, 4, 16

G
growing up, 4

L
lifeguard, 18

M
medicine, 16

N
neighborhood, 8, 9

P
parents, 4, 11, 14,
    20–21
poison, 10

S
safety rules, 22
    bicycle, 8–9
    fire and electrical,
        10–11
    swimming, 18
    traffic, 8–9
scared, being, 4, 14
strangers, 12